HOT MAMA'S
EROTIC COOKERY

Hot Mama's Erotic Cookery

Spicy Recipes for the Shameless Sybarite

Susan F Edwards

Cover design by Syneca Featherstone at OriginalSyn

Dedicated to the original Hot Mama

"I'll try anything once, twice if I like it, three times to make sure."
~ *Mae West*

Accolades for *Hot Mama's Erotic Cookery*

"This book should be banned, burned and then buried somewhere far from decent people, maybe New York."
~Ron DeSantis, Governor of Florida, Defender of Innocence

"A heartbreaking work of staggering genius. Oh, wait, that's a whole different book. I didn't actually read this one. Looks like it's for chicks."
~Seymour Butz, Goodreads Critic

"Disgusting, dirty and downright trashy. She should be ashamed of herself. But those cheese grits are good with Merlot."
~Penelope Pursey, Mom Blogger

"Frankly, I was a little disappointed. I thought it needed more sex and some pictures of naked men."
~Eileen Dover, Loyal Romance Reader

"Meh."
~Taylor Cole, Author, *Aphrodisiac Cookbook for Angry Women*

Author's Note

This cookbook has been a long time coming. Almost 40 years to be exact. Noel Smith and I had already been cooking together for a few years — and making earth-mother-type Christmas presents for our friends and families — herbal sachets, pot pies, salad dressings, that sort of thing. They were big fun and a huge amount of work. And in the case of the salad dressings, nearly lethal.

We hit on herb-spice blends in 1991 and have been making an annual batch ever since.

We talked about doing a cookbook for several years but never quite got around to it. We always envisioned the character of Hot Mama as a fun-loving, sensual bon vivant. When I was hired by erotic romance book publisher Ellora's Cave to start a magazine devoted to women's sexuality, I asked Noel for permission to use Hot Mama's name for a cooking column. Noel agreed and, because it was, after all, a magazine about sex, the monthly column featured a considerably more wanton Hot Mama than we originally envisioned. Most of the recipes in this book are slightly toned-down versions of those columns I wrote for *Lady Jaided* magazine from 2005 through 2009.

Noel bought the signature Hot Mama red high heel for $2.99 at a Salvation Army on Nebraska Avenue in Tampa.

Almost everything in this book is fictional, entirely the product of an overheated imagination fueled by copious amounts of good food and wine and the occasional cigar.

We hope you enjoy Hot Mama's naughty escapades and the recipes we have evolved over many years of cooking for the people we love.

Susan Edwards
Tampa, Florida, 2023

The Maid of Honor's Toast

I hate waking up in strange places. Especially gritty ones. This one was, by the looks of it, a sand trap.

So many questions leapt to mind as I opened one eye and ran a dry tongue over the parched landscape of my mouth: How did I get here? When did I learn to play golf? Where are my shoes? What's for lunch?

I stood up just in time to hear someone shout, "Fore!" and dove back into the sand. The ball whizzed past my head, missing it by inches.

Maybe the impact jarred my memory. Or maybe it was the feel of the cool sand against my stomach.

My *bare* stomach — and legs …

Uh oh.

Suddenly the memory of last night's little bachelorette shebang flashed before my eyes. Patsy Rose's last night as a single cowgirl. A bunch of us doing shots of tequila in the back of her pickup truck and singing Amy Winehouse songs. It didn't seem sporting to just leer at the handsome stripper we hired while he peeled off his cop costume, so we all played a game of strip golf with croquet mallets on the public course down the street.

Now here I was, in bra and panties, waving off the apologies of an elderly golfer who was either almost blind or too polite to acknowledge what I wasn't wearing.

A glance at his watch told me I had an hour to shower, put on my maid of honor dress and get myself to the church on time.

I needed a major morning-after antidote. Pair this Bloody Mary with avocado toast, and you will be a new woman.

Seriously Bloody Mary

2 ½ oz. tomato juice
Juice of ¼ lime
Dash of Crystal Hot Sauce or sriracha
Dash of Worcestershire sauce
Pinch of horseradish
1 ½ oz. vodka

Serve over ice in a tall, salt-rimmed glass with a fresh, crunchy stalk of celery, a lime wedge, or large green olives speared with a cocktail pick. If you're in a hurry or just don't feel like making a project of it, Mr. T's or Zing Zang Bloody Mary Mix works just fine.

Drink two before you even think about looking in the mirror.

Arabian Nights

Omar said he was a prince and I had no reason to doubt him. A man with that many wives must have some royal coffers to keep them in Ferragamos and silk. I met him on a flight to Egypt, and he told me with a sly smile that he had six wives.

"Does it disgust you," he asked, probing me with a smoldering gaze, "the idea a that man can love so many women?"

"Not at all," I replied, letting my nostrils flare just a bit. "The question is, can man *satisfy* so many women?"

He laughed loud and long at this and insisted I come to his home for dinner. "You can find out for yourself," he said.

It was an invitation I couldn't refuse.

The answer is yes, with the right skills and attitude, a man can satisfy any number of women over and over again.

Omar brought all seven of us to moaning simultaneous satisfaction with this fabulous dish he learned from his grandmother.

Cooked this long, the garlic loses all its sharp-edged taste and takes on a sweet, mellow, nutty flavor. The smell alone is enough to send some people right over the edge.

Chicken with 40 Cloves of Garlic

3 tablespoons olive oil
1 tablespoon butter
3 pounds boneless, skinless chicken thighs
40 cloves of garlic (or two full heads), peeled
2 tablespoons lemon juice (or juice of one lemon)
1 teaspoon salt
½ teaspoon thyme
½ teaspoon Hot Mama Casbah
¼ teaspoon ground black pepper
¼ cup water

Preheat oven to 350°.

Heat oil and butter over medium heat in Dutch oven or other large, heavy pot with lid. Add chicken and brown, about 5 minutes per side.

Add garlic and stir, then add lemon juice, salt, pepper, thyme Hot Mama and water.

Cover and bake 1½ to 2 hours.

Serves 4-6

Two to Tango

There are lots of ways to tell what kind of lover a man will be before you find yourself having to climb out his bathroom window after Mr. Hunk in the bar turns out to be Mr. Clunky in the sack.

Everyone knows you can tell a lot from the way a man kisses. But once a man gets to first base, he already has expectations, putting you in a potentially sticky situation. The earlier you know his sexual IQ, the less time you'll waste and the fewer sneaky retreats you'll have to beat.

Certain places present opportunities to glean the information you need. I often shop for carnal companionship at the grocery store, where I can see what a man likes to eat and how he squeezes the melons and sniffs the cheeses.

Oyster bars are also good spots to size up a catch before casting your net. All you have to do is sit and watch to see who passes the oyster test, then pick the one you like best. In case you don't know, the oyster test is really quite simple. If a man eats an oyster with gusto, chances are, he'll be an enthusiastic cunnilinguist, though it doesn't necessarily attest to his skill.

But one of my favorite places to gauge a man's sexual prowess is on the dance floor. Dancing is like making love with your clothes on. And Latin dancing is the most seductive of all. The drama and passion of the tango, the sensual rhythms of marimba and meringue, the delicious tease of salsa and cha cha cha get my blood going like nothing else.

That's why when I want a really sensual lover, someone to seduce me with finesse and fire, I go to my favorite Latin dance club. It also happens to serve a delicious chicken dish you won't find anywhere else. It's sweet and savory and thoroughly delicious with yellow rice, though I often serve it with quinoa and pineapple. It's also incredibly easy to make.

Tango Thighs

3 pounds of boneless, skinless chicken thighs
2 teaspoons cinnamon
¼ cup honey
¼ cup chicken broth
½ cup sherry
3 tablespoons fresh lime juice
1-2 garlic cloves, minced
Salt and pepper to taste

Arrange chicken in baking dish and sprinkle with cinnamon.

Combine remaining ingredients in a bowl and pour over chicken, keeping back 2 tablespoons of lime juice.

Preheat oven to 375°F and bake 1 hour, basting frequently with pan juices. Sprinkle with remaining lime juice before serving.

Can't Beat This Meat

Red meat brings out the beast in a man. So when my animal side gets restless, I pay a visit to Bob, my friendly neighborhood butcher. Bob's inner beast needs no waking; it's on the prowl pretty much all the time. Maybe working around all that blood and muscle raises the predator in a man. Or maybe a certain type of person is drawn to knives and cleavers.

All I know is that when I walk into Bob's House of Meats, he locks those cold, gray eyes on me, and suddenly I'm a wildebeest caught on an open plain. The back of my neck prickles and the little hairs rise. Blood rushes to my face.

Bob bares his teeth in what barely passes for a smile. He doesn't laugh so much as growl. Whenever I go into his shop, he licks his lips and asks what he can do for me.

If I have the time, I might ask him to take me back to the cooler and show me what he's got. Otherwise, I just have him cut me steaks from whatever's fresh and nicely marbled with fat. I like my steaks at least an inch thick so I can get the outside seared and the fat crispy without overcooking the inside. I eat mine rare, but I'll give it to a guest any way he wants it.

Beastly Good Steak

Before cooking, I sprinkle the steaks generously with kosher salt, a little rosemary, and coarsely ground black pepper.

For rare steak, you've got to get the fire hot, and the meat close to it. If you're broiling, put the rack up high enough so the meat is no more than four inches from the heat source. For grilling, use plenty of charcoal, and put the steaks on as soon as the coals ash over, while they're at their hottest. For rare steaks, grill for five minutes, flip and grill another five minutes. Add about three minutes per side for each degree of doneness.

Any old cook might just slap the meat on a plate and serve it sizzling hot when it's done. If it's a good cut and cooked right, it'll be delicious just like that. But if you want it to be truly memorable—if you want it to wake up the beast and make him howl—take just another few minutes for this simple but orgasmic finish.

Once the steak is done, put it on a warmed plate and let it sit for a few minutes so the juices gather. Then pour the juice into a shallow pan. Add ¼ cup of red wine. Cook on medium heat until the liquid is reduced by about half, usually 5 to 7 minutes. Add a large pat or two of butter and swirl it in the pan until melted. Pour over steaks.

You should serve this only to a man you really like because he will stalk you like a hungry wolf forever after he gets a taste of it.

A Jug of Wine, a Loaf of Bread, and Sven

I met Sven at the cheese-tasting counter in my favorite gourmet food shop. He was sniffing a tart little piece of Buchrondin, a strong, earthy, hard goat's milk cheese. He popped the morsel in his mouth and let out a small moan of pleasure. The bulge in his tight little bicycle shorts told me this might be a man who could appreciate my cooking.

But I'm not easy. I don't cook for just anyone—even a blond, muscled god in purple bicycle shorts with flames on the crotch.

Sven had to prove himself worthy of my culinary talents before I was going to give him a taste of my kitchen.

"You like that cheese?" I asked him. Cool as a cucumber.

He grinned and nodded, shuffling the impressive lump in his shorts to a more comfortable position.

"How about this one?" I asked, picking up a sliver of Manchego. It's a yummy, nutty Spanish cheese that everyone loves.

He ate it from my hand, licking my fingers thoroughly and never taking his eyes off mine.

"Tasty," he said in a cool Nordic accent, "But a little bit tame. I want something that teases my tongue."

"Like this," he said, picking up a snowy mound of Cabrales on a slice of crusty baguette and placing it in my mouth. It was my turn to moan. This rich, stinky Spanish blend made of cow's, goat's, and sheep's milk, with thick veins of musty blue cheese tastes like good sex feels. Randy and delicious.

"I have a 2003 bottle of Castle Rock pinot noir at my house," he whispered in my ear. It's not expensive as pinot noir goes, under $20. But it's got a full berry taste that does something wonderful in your mouth with a good cheese.

Here was a man who could appreciate what I had to offer—and who could give as good as he got. I nearly jumped into his shopping cart.

Since then, Sven and I have shared many oral pleasures. But we always come back to the first menu that brought us together. It's the perfect recipe for a picnic seduction, inside or out.

Three-Cheese Picnic

¼ lb Buchrondin cheese
¼ lb Cabrales cheese
¼ lb Manchego cheese
2 bottles Castle Rock Pinot Noir
1 French baguette
1 knife, 1 corkscrew, 2 cloth napkins
1 blanket

Bundle all ingredients into a large basket and find a meadow, back yard, or — in case of inclement weather — an open stretch of carpet. Spread blanket. Open wine. Proceed from there.

Adam's Juicy Peaches

There's something about a plump, ripe peach. So round, so soft, so sweet and succulent. The downy skin and rosy cleft so lovely and inviting. It was August, and I was cruising a country road in Georgia, heart of peach land, hunting for just the right roadside stand at which to score the perfect peaches. Just the thought of biting into a sweet, juicy Georgia peach fresh off a tree had my mouth watering, and I was getting impatient.

It had been too long since I'd had a good peach, but that was no reason to lower my standards. In fact, it made me even choosier than usual, so I passed several uninviting stands manned by rough-skinned, scowling farmers. Buying fresh fruit and vegetables should be a pleasurable, sensual experience, not a parched exchange with an unattractive stranger on a dusty road.

When I came upon a neatly painted stand in a shady grove, I was glad I'd held out. Hand-painted fruits and vegetables adorned the sign, flanking the words "Adam's Garden Produce."

Beneath the sign sat beautiful young Adam, looking like he'd just been expelled from the Garden of Eden and was doing his best to replicate it here amongst us sinners. I wondered where Eve had gone off to as I surveyed Adam's glossy chestnut curls and broad, sun-kissed shoulders.

I thought young Adam might be naked at first or wearing a fig leaf. But when I peeked over the counter to get a better look at his zucchini, I discovered with some disappointment that he was wearing snug jeans slung low on his lean, muscled groin.

Ah, but soon enough in the grove behind his stand, I sampled all of sweet Adam's wares. And as the moon rose over the grove, I was thoroughly sated and happily on my way with a bushel of fresh peaches.

This luscious salad always brings fond memories of Adam's downy skin and juicy peaches and the day I had my fill of both.

If your peaches are not quite ripe, spritz 'em with walnut oil and bake (at 400°F) or grill them, cut side down, until they soften and carmelize, cool, then peel and slice.

Peaches and Cream Salad

2 ripe peaches, thinly sliced
2 tablespoons walnut oil
2 tablespoons cream
2 tablespoons lemon juice
1 head of romaine lettuce
2 cups arugula (optional)
3 tablespoons chopped fresh chives (optional)

Peel peaches or just rub fuzz off the skins and slice thin.

Place peach slices and greens (lettuce, arugula, chives) in a large bowl, sprinkle with lemon juice, and toss briskly until juice is evenly distributed.

Whisk together walnut oil and cream and season with salt and pepper.

Pour dressing over salad, toss and serve.

Franco's Secret

Franco owns my favorite little Italian bistro in town. Being a tad on the under-groomed side for my tastes, he's never been terribly attractive to me. But he's a madly talented chef and a nice enough man so I let him kiss my cheek and get away with copping the occasional "accidental" feel.

Everything he makes is exquisite, but I'm especially fond of his penne with vodka sauce. It's creamy, delicious and very satisfying.

Franco learned to cook from his grandma in the old country and he's very secretive about his family recipes. But I can be relentless when it comes to getting what I want. I begged. I beseeched. I flattered and cajoled.

At last, he consented. On one condition. I had to let him make love to me. Only once, he said, but he would call all the shots, where, when — and exactly what we would do.

Well, for you, dear reader, I was prepared to make the sacrifice. That's the kind of Hot Mama I am. You know I'm not one to kiss and tell, so I can't give you details. Let's just say the man has a well-equipped kitchen and he knows how to use it. I'll never look at a spatula the same way again.

Franco's Penne With Vodka Sauce

1 tablespoon extra virgin olive oil
1 small sweet onion, chopped
6 roma tomatoes, peeled, seeded, and crushed or 1 can crushed
tomatoes (28 oz., no flavoring added please!)
½ teaspoon of sugar (if you're using fresh tomatoes)
¼ cup vodka
¾ cup cream
1 pound penne pasta, cooked according to directions on package
½ teaspoon Hot Mama

Saute onion in evoo in skillet over medium-low heat until soft
and translucent, 5-10 minutes. Do not brown.

Add tomatoes and sugar. Simmer 20-30 minutes until sauce
thickens.

Add vodka, salt and pepper and simmer another 10 minutes
until alcohol is cooked off.

Allow sauce to cool and then puree until smooth.

Return pureed sauce to pan, add cream, stirring to blend, and
heat slowly over medium low. Do not allow to boil. Toss with
cooked penne and serve.

Preparation note: Franco would never consider using canned
tomatoes but I think they work just fine in this dish. If you do use
fresh, you must peel them first. It's quick and easy. Just place
tomatoes in a big bowl or pot, pour boiling water over them and
let them sit for about a minute. The skins will slip off easily.

Also if you want a less rich but still satisfying version,
substitute evaporated milk or fat-free yogurt for cream. If you use
yogurt, mix it with some of the cooled, pureed tomato mixture
before adding to the pan to avoid lumping.

The Beet Goes On

Hot Mama loves red food. Beets, tomatoes, red peppers, cherries, and rare steak all titillate my taste buds and make me feel like Popeye on a spinach high. Especially beets, one of nature's most incredible foods, packed with nutrition and flavor. If your experience of beets is confined to those from a can or jar, you are missing most of their charm, flavor and tonic effects.

I regularly roast beets (skin on for two hours at 350°F) and put them in salads or just slice, drizzle with oil and vinegar, and eat as a side dish in place of dull ol' taters.

Every self-respecting beet freak and Slav has at least one borscht recipe. There are as many borscht recipes as there are babushka-wearing mamas, inspired free-form cooks like me and fusion interpreters like Vlad, the chef at my favorite Romanian restaurant in Miami. He has half a dozen borscht recipes, all completely different.

Vlad's borschts range from beefy and chunky to refined and creamy, and even crystalline, like liquid rubies.

This one is rich and sweet, a little rustic. It is best served hot and is even more flavorful if made the day before serving. The color is stunning and will scare the hell out of the culinarily timid and people with a blood phobia. However, the iron-rich sweetness of this dish and its blood-red color are hugely attractive and satisfying to vampires, carnivores and vegans alike.

Vlad's New World Borscht

3 medium beets
1 medium onion
1 stalk celery
1 small to medium red bell pepper
1 cup mushrooms
1 large Granny Smith apple
2 tablespoons butter
2 tablespoons vegetable oil
1-2 teaspoons salt
1 teaspoon black pepper
½ teaspoon cumin
½ teaspoon thyme
1 bay leaf
Juice from 1/2 a lemon or lime
10 cups vegetable, beef or chicken broth

Wash beets and trim off greens, leaving a half-inch of stem. Make sure not to puncture the skin or cut root at the bottom of beet or it will dry up and bleed out all that wonderful sugar that makes it so sweet. Roast 1 hour at 400°F. Cool for an hour, peel and chop.

Chop rest of vegetables, mushrooms and apple and place in a large saucepan or stock pot with oil, butter and 2-4 tablespoons of broth. Cover and cook over low-medium heat for 15 minutes. Add beets and spices and stir to coat and heat through, 3-5 minutes. Add citrus juice and broth, bring to a boil and cook for 5 minutes. Lower heat, cover and simmer for another 30 minutes.

Cool for one hour, remove bay leaf and blend in blender or food processor until smooth. Reheat and serve with a sprinkle of toasted breadcrumbs, a big, swirly dollop of sour cream or plain rustic Greek yogurt and a few sprigs of fresh or a sprinkle of dried dill.

Turkish Delight

When it comes to lovers, Hot Mama believes fervently that multiculturalism is the spice of life. Ayaz was Turkish and he enjoyed making love in short bouts several times a night. In between rounds, he liked to bathe and then have a bite to eat— nothing too heavy, just something to stir the senses and fortify the constitution. Sometimes it was just a handful of dates and nuts or a sweet pastry.

Often, one of the courses would be savory Turkish-style roasted vegetables. His cook had endless variations, adding whatever leftover vegetables she had, but this is her basic recipe.

It makes an excellent dip, appetizer, vegetarian main dish or side dish for meat, chicken or fish. It can be made with all kinds of vegetables, although you want to avoid the watery ones. I love it with butternut squash.

It is perfumed with sumac, a Mediterranean spice that has a tangy, lemony flavor. Lemon zest can be substituted for the sumac, which can be found in Middle Eastern grocery stores and over the internet.

Roasted Vegetable Salad

1 medium eggplant cut into 1-inch cubes
1 large onion diced
1 green and 1 red or yellow bell pepper cut into 1-inch pieces
2 large carrots sliced
3 or 4 cloves of garlic, skinned, whole (more if you love garlic)
2 cups whole grape tomatoes
Virgin olive oil spray
1 tablespoon sumac powder or substitute lemon zest
Salt, pepper
Fresh parsley, chopped
1/3 cup chopped walnuts

Spray shallow roasting pans with oil spray or slick with olive oil; add vegetables, one or two types per pan. Keep them separate, though, as different vegetables roast at different rates. Spray with more oil to lightly coat.

Put in preheated 350°F oven and roast, turning occasionally, until soft and uniformly golden. Place roasted vegetables in bowl, add seasonings and adjust to your taste. You can also add any bits and pieces of already cooked vegetables you have

This dish can be made ahead of time and stored in the refrigerator for up to two days. It is best served at room temperature. To serve, mound in center of decorative plate, drizzle with oil, and sprinkle with walnuts and fresh parsley.

Serve with wedges of pita, flatbread, crackers or lavash.

Revenge of the Sea Captain

The last time I saw my handsome Brazilian sea captain Alejandro was almost a year ago. He was cursing my name and vowing to get even with me for tying him up and serving chilled oysters on his naked body to my sister Nicole. But that was only payback after he stood me up for a date on New Year's Eve.

I was a little suspicious when he called last month to say he was in town for a few days and ask me to meet him for a drink. That deep voice and syncopated accent reminded me of his strong hands and sure lips and the way he'd rocked me all night long in the captain's quarters on his ship. How could I refuse?

With his curly, dark hair and smoldering eyes, he was every bit as hot as I remembered, and after two drinks, I was more than ready to retire to the captain's quarters.

I guess I should have seen it coming.

After riding the waves of passion all night long, I awoke late the next morning to discover we were far out to sea. I managed to jump ship at a small port in Chile and ended up in a small village in the Andes mountains.

That's where I discovered quinoa (pronounced keen-wa). It's a delicious, nutritious tiny grain that dates back to the Incas. It's also easy to prepare and incredibly versatile. It cooks in 15 minutes and can take the place of rice, pasta and other grains in main dishes, side dishes, salads—even desserts. It comes in all colors from light golden to red and purple.

I was surprised to learn when I finally got back home that you can find it at most local grocery stores in the organics or pasta section.

This dish is colorful, delicious, nutritious and filling. Plus, it can be prepared a day in advance.

Inca Party Salad

1 cup dry golden quinoa (yields 3-4 cups after being cooked)
1 cup sliced carrots lightly steamed until just al dente
1 small sweet onion diced
1 red bell pepper diced
1 green bell pepper diced
1 cucumber sliced
1 cup fresh cooked sweet corn

Dressing:
¼ cup olive oil
Juice of one lime
Salt and pepper to taste

Prepare quinoa according to directions on package and set aside to cool.

Whisk together olive oil and lime juice and toss with vegetables and cooled quinoa. Serve chilled or at room temperature.

You can do endless variations on this recipe, using different vegetables, beans, cheeses, fruits, nuts and dressings.

How to Handle a Hungry Pirate

I want to reassure you right up front that tales of my abduction by pirates in the Devil's Triangle are vastly exaggerated. Cap'n Jimmy says he was covering for me, but the truth is he was too embarrassed to tell my editor what really happened when she called him and demanded to know my whereabouts. Though I was not kidnapped, I did end up on a pirate ship and honestly could not help missing the deadline for this month's column. I blame Cap'n Jimmy, who ran aground on a sandbar off a small Caribbean island on the way to a wedding in Grenada.

We soon discovered we had gotten ourselves stranded in prime hunting waters for a band of seagoing marauders known as Los Gasparillos. It didn't take long for them to find us. Jimmy's boat is not lavish, but they boarded us anyway and tore the boat apart, looking for money, "square grouper," or anything else of value.

Things were looking bad for Cap'n Jimmy and me. We'd both heard plenty of tales of sailors murdered by pirates, and this band looked like they wouldn't hesitate to slit our throats. Jimmy doesn't believe in guns and wouldn't let me bring even my little Rossi .38 pistol onboard. So, without a firearm, there was only one thing I could think of to do.

Even the most savage beast can be tamed with food and a bit of maternal moxie, so while they were tossing the place, I started to cook.

I mashed some garlic cloves and tossed them in a pan with about a quarter cup of olive oil over a medium flame, adding a tablespoon of fermented black beans, which sound gross but are actually wonderful smoky-flavored pebbles that add depth, flavor and saltiness to dishes. The explosion of smell filled the cabin, grabbing the pirates by the nose and drawing them to the galley.

Jimmy had caught some gorgeous redfish that day, so I cut them into bite-size pieces and tossed them in the oil. (You could use any firm-fleshed fish or seafood, including tuna, grouper, scallops, shrimp or a combination thereof.)

I threw in a dash of the hot pepper and herb blend I make myself and take everywhere. (You can substitute a pinch of savory herbs and a slap of hot red pepper flakes or ground cayenne, or even a bit of finely diced jalapeno). I tossed it all together for a few minutes while the pirates looked over my shoulder, salivating.

When the fish was done, I removed it with a spatula and laid it on a bed of cold corkscrew pasta, spritzing the whole thing generously with lime juice and sprinkling with capers. (Picnic, party and sailing hint: You can make pasta ahead of time, toss it with a bit of oil and freeze or chill it for future use. Quinoa is even easier and more nutritious to use this way.)

To the remaining pan juices, I added a dollop of butter and a half cup of white wine, lowered the heat just a bit and let it cook down.

By this time, I had the pirates almost literally eating out of my hand, so I pressed my advantage. I ordered one to set the table, another to serve drinks and a third to get the chilled asparagus salad from the cooler. I even made them join hands around the table while I said grace.

By the time dinner was over, we knew each other's names, and the pirate leader, Carlos, had agreed to take me to Grenada. Cap'n Jimmy stayed with his ship, waiting for high waters to release him from the sandbar. By the time he was freed, it was too late to make the wedding, so he sailed home.

I didn't make it in time for the wedding either. Turns out, pirates are not all that dependable about keeping to a schedule or even a destination for that matter, especially when a marauding opportunity presents itself.

In the end, it wasn't all that big a deal that we missed the wedding. So did the bride. (Long story). The only one who was really put out was that uptight editor.

Bite My Peaches

I often find my lovers in grocery stores because that's where people reveal their sensual sides without even knowing it. I'll take a plain man sniffing a melon and gently pressing its surface to test for ripeness any day over an Adonis who's tossing frozen dinners into his buggy.

Fruits are among the most sensual of foods, and you can tell a lot about a man by the way he approaches nature's sweetest offerings. If a man has no appreciation for the soft blushing flesh of a peach, its sumptuous cleft and slick, juicy interior, what makes you think he's going to eat your papaya with any gusto?

If you haven't decided yet whether a certain someone is worth taking to your boudoir, you might try my favorite easy peach recipe. It will turn even the most hardened fruit-disdainer into a peach-licking, cherry-sucking sybarite before your very eyes.

If it doesn't, tell him you've got to get up early and send him on his way.

Hot Stuffed Peaches

¼ cup chopped toasted pecans
6 tablespoons turbinado (or brown) sugar
1 tablespoon grated orange peel
6 peaches, pitted and cut in half
½ cup sherry

Preheat oven to 350° and place peach halves, skin side down, in a baking dish.

Combine half the sugar with the pecans and orange peel and spoon the mixture into the peach halves. Sprinkle with remaining sugar and sherry. Bake 10-15 minutes and serve warm with whipped cream or ice cream.

Hot Mama's Secret

For Kevin Goehring

Hot Mama's good friend, Bachelor Biff, used to always say, "If you want chocolate cake, you've got to ask for chocolate cake." I know he was being metaphorical, but I always thought that if you wanted chocolate cake you had to *make* chocolate cake—even metaphorically.

Bachelor Biff is a bit of a princess, though, so I just chalked up the difference to his talent for getting other people to do things for him.

Then I saw *The Secret*. Sure enough, these weirdly happy people said, you just have to ask for something, imagine already having it, *taste* the chocolate mocha frosting in your mind as though the cake has just materialized on a pretty china plate in the kitchen.

Apparently, learning to do this can take some time, though. In the meantime, here's a recipe for chocolate cake, in case you get a hankering for a piece before you learn to manifest it. Come to think of it, maybe that's how *The Secret* really works. If you want something bad enough to taste it, you can't get it out of your head until you just go out and get you some—any way you can.

I've never had a chocolate cake appear just because I wanted one. But I have had a handsome man appear just as I'm taking one out of the oven. Which brings me to one of the best secrets I know for attracting what you want: Find out what it likes to eat and make it. Everything else just follows naturally.

Secret Chocolate Cake

½ cup butter softened at room temperature
2 cups brown sugar
2 eggs beaten
½ cup buttermilk
½ cup warm water with 1 teaspoon soda dissolved in it
2 cups flour sifted with ¼ teaspoon baking powder
2 squares baker's chocolate, melted
1 teaspoon vanilla extract

Preheat oven to 350°F. Grease two nine-inch cake pans and sprinkle with sugar.

In a large bowl, cream together the butter and sugar. Add flour in small amounts, alternating with eggs, milk and water and beating until smooth in between.

Add chocolate and vanilla and mix well.

Pour into oiled pans and bake 30 minutes.

Chocolate Mocha Frosting

3 cups confectioner sugar
3 tablespoons butter
5-6 tablespoons strong brewed coffee chilled
6 teaspoons dry cocoa
1 teaspoon vanilla

Cream together the sugar and butter, adding coffee gradually to soften the mixture. Add cocoa and vanilla and mix thoroughly.

Chef's Table for One

Hot Mama confesses to special tingly feelings for Emeril Lagasse. Watching his cooking show is like hanging out in his kitchen and having him seduce you with food and music.

It's just true that a man in an apron is sexy, and there's nothing hotter than a man at the stove. Even a homely man looks beautiful when he's cooking up a special dish just for you.

Take Iron Chef Bobby Flay. He's a whole different kind of sexy from Emeril. Bobby, I could see spending some time with. Emeril would have to leave by noon the next day — after round three or four of raucous, rambunctious *amore*.

Of course, I'd have him whip me up an omelet first and then maybe come back to bed for a couple more rounds. But he'd have to be gone by 4 p.m., I swear. By then I'd probably be sick of him yelling "Kick it up a notch!" and "Bam!"

This recipe is my variation of one he did with shrimp and fish, which was as spicy and tasty as the man himself. But I can't give you his recipe because he might sue me. In which case he might never cook me dinner and then breakfast.

Thighs Wide Open

(for Emeril)

1 lb. skinless chicken thighs
1 cup each of sweet red pepper and green bell pepper cut in chunks
Half cup of olives
1 cup onions
½ cup sliced fennel bulb (substitution: celery)
Six roma tomatoes, chopped (or a 14 oz. can chopped tomatoes)
2 tablespoons tomato paste
Parsley, thyme and bay leaf, chopped basil, minced garlic, all preferably fresh
Salt, cayenne
Dash of Worcestershire sauce
Hot sauce, preferably Crystal Hot Sauce or sriracha
2-3 tablespoons olive oil
One 14-oz. can of chicken broth (or better yet, homemade).

In a large Dutch oven, heat 2 tablespoons olive oil over medium heat and brown chicken (5-10 minutes per side) Remove chicken and set aside.

Add another tablespoon of oil if necessary and stir in pepper, onions, fennel, salt and cayenne. Toss in oil for 2-3 minutes and add garlic. When garlic is browned, add tomatoes and stir in tomato paste. Add parsley, thyme, basil, Worcestershire sauce, hot sauce and chicken broth and bring to boil.

Add chicken and olives, reduce heat, cover and stew over low heat for 30 to 45 minutes, until chicken is fall-off-the-bone tender.

Serve with crusty French bread. Did I mention it's low fat?

Come to Mama

A broken foot has laid Hot Mama low for several weeks. (A word to the wise: Take off those heels before attempting to join the mile-high club in a DC-9 lavatory.)

So I've been watching more cooking shows on television with my foot propped up on a pillow and a glass of wine in my hand.

I've always had the hots for Emeril, and now I'm falling for Nigella. The way her ample breasts bounce and quiver when she beats egg whites into a froth or kneads a knob of dough seems to whisper, "Come to mama."

I picture her turning up at my house, cooing comforting words over my throbbing foot and unpacking a basket of food. I've never seen her make this dish, otherwise known as piccata, but it's my favorite way to treat tender white breasts. I usually call it Hot Mama's Succulent Breasts, but if she ever cooked it for me, I'd change the name forever in her honor.

Nigella's Succulent Breasts

1 lb. boneless, skinless chicken breasts, pounded to ½ inch
thickness
2 tablespoons capers
2 tablespoons white wine
2 tablespoons chicken broth
2 tablespoons flour
1teaspoon salt
3-4 tablespoons olive oil
1 tablespoon lemon juice

Dredge chicken in flour and salt. Heat olive oil in frying pan
over medium heat and add chicken. Cook 4-6 minutes per side, till
browned and chicken is cooked through.

Remove chicken. Stir in wine and broth and cook 2 minutes,
scraping up the browned bits of flour. Add capers and lemon juice,
and return chicken to pan. Heat through and serve.

From Russia, with Love

I first saw him on the midnight train from Moscow to St. Petersburg one cold, snowy February night. He was smoking cigarettes and drinking vodka, and staring out the window into the dark landscape. His steel gray hair was thick and curly on top and neatly razored on the sides and back. His face had strong, sensual features: deep-set eyes, a prominent brow ridge, substantial Roman nose, full shapely lips, and a sturdy jaw.

Well-worn jeans and a black leather jacket sculpted his lanky frame nicely but didn't do much to shield him from the bone-chilling Russian winter. He wasn't famous yet, but I recognized him from the author picture on his first book.

He shivered and looked a little melancholy, so I sent him a plate of caviar and black bread to go with his vodka. We ended up forgoing the bread and eating the caviar Russian style: placing a dollop on the back of the hand and licking it off each other's knuckles, chased by a shot of vodka.

Everyone should make love on a train at least once. No ship, no airplane, no automobile hurtling down a highway can match the sheer power of a locomotive pounding down the tracks.

Since then, our paths have crossed occasionally, over *kefteh* in the vast Arabian desert, *mole rojo* in a lovely Oaxacan courtyard cafe, and a picnic of *tortilla de patata* and *rioja* wine high in the mountains of Catalonia. But whenever I have vodka and caviar, I think of making hot, locomotive love on a cold Russian winter night.

The simplest, most Russian and most sensual way to enjoy caviar calls for only two ingredients: iced vodka and caviar.

The success of this dish is all in the ingredients and the ritual of consumption. Since this is really a dish for two, splurge on quality; you don't need a large quantity. Remember that metal imparts an undesirable flavor to caviar, so use bone, pearl or even plastic spoons to serve it.

First, put the vodka and some shot glasses in the freezer for at least four hours before serving.

People who say they don't like caviar have probably never had decent caviar, and they probably neglected to chase it with a shot of good vodka. The rarest caviar, even in small quantities is hugely expensive, but there are several kinds of good caviar that won't cost you a week's pay.

Don't bother trying to buy beluga, the Cadillac of caviars, since overfishing has rendered its source—sturgeon in the Caspian Sea—nearly extinct. It's illegal now, so any beluga you order is either not real beluga, illegally obtained, or not very fresh. Here's the lowdown on a few of the more common ones you can enjoy without guilt:

Osetra Caviar: If you're going to eat it straight, it's best to get the good stuff, and Osetra is the good stuff. It runs $70-150 an ounce. Rich, buttery and slightly sweet, this juicy, gray, medium-grained caviar is silky, smooth and delicious all by itself. In fact, you'll miss all its subtle flavor transitions if you put anything on it.

Bowfin Caviar: This is what the average American probably thinks of when caviar is mentioned. These tiny shiny black eggs burst on the tongue with a salty, fishy flavor and taste great all by themselves or as a garnish. At around $12 for a couple of ounces, it's cheap and plentiful enough to allow you to splurge on high-end vodka or Champagne, both of which pair perfectly with caviar. Jackie Kennedy's favorite dinner is said to have been a baked potato with caviar and a glass of Champagne. This would be fabulous for that meal. All I would add for a romantic dinner would be a dollop of sour cream or crème fraiche (recipe below) and a lush green salad.

Paddlefish Caviar: Incredibly inexpensive at around $15 an ounce, this fine-grain, gray caviar is surprisingly smooth and refined. Rich and nutty with sweet, earthy and salty notes, it is good by itself too. It has a stronger flavor than the more expensive caviars, though, so you might enjoy it more on toast points with just as squeeze of lemon or a tiny dollop of sour cream or crème fraiche (recipe on next page).

Golden Whitefish Roe: For my taste, this roe from a species of salmon found in the Great Lakes is too fishy and intense to eat alone. Instead, these gorgeous tiny golden orange eggs make a lovely garnish for a baked potato, an omelet or deviled eggs. At less than $10 for a four-ounce jar, it adds an inexpensive touch of elegance and dash of flavor to bland food. Regular salmon roe is much larger grained and too slimy and fishy even as a garnish for me. If you like the taste of salmon, go for golden whitefish roe instead.

Crème Fraiche

Even if you don't like caviar, crème fraiche is a delicious and ridiculously easy-to-make, decadent staple of French cooking that can be used in hundreds of ways. Like sour cream but richer and sweeter with a velvety texture, it's delicious dolloped on pies, cakes, puddings, cobblers, fruit salads, potatoes, and soups. It's also used as a thickener for soups and sauces.

1 cup heavy cream
2 tablespoons buttermilk
Combine in a glass jar and let stand at room temperature until it thickens (8-24 hours) then refrigerate.

Body and Soul Food

Hard Times have officially arrived at Casa Hot Mama and we're pinching every penny 'til it weeps for mercy. Groceries have gotten so expensive that I've been reduced to trading my, uh, cooking services in exchange for a decent bottle of wine or two and some artisan cheese.

Fortunately, I grew up on soul food, so I know how make the most out of grains, beans and bones. Bread is outrageously expensive, and most of the stuff in you get in the grocery store is bland in flavor and texture, not to mention largely devoid of nutritional value.

That's why, when the going gets tough, the tough make their own bread. But don't worry, I'm not going to have you begging yeast to grow and kneading gooey globs of dough. Quick breads are easy, inexpensive, delicious and nutritious, and cornbread is one of the most filling and versatile of all quick breads.

My mama and her mama before her thought nothing of whipping up a batch of cornbread to eat with beans for dinner, with butter and molasses for dessert, and crumbled up in milk for breakfast. Whenever there was nothing else to eat, there was always cornbread.

Hot Mama's Mama's Cornbread

2 eggs beaten
1-1 1/3 cups buttermilk (in a pinch use regular milk with a
tablespoon of vinegar added)
1 cup yellow cornmeal
1 cup all-purpose flour
¼ cup oil or shortening
2 teaspoons baking powder
Dash of salt

Preheat oven to 400°F. Combine egg, buttermilk, salt, baking
powder, flour and cornmeal and mix well. Heat oil or shortening
in nine-inch cast iron skillet over medium heat or in the oven
while it heats. When heated through, pour half of the oil from the
pan into the cornmeal mixture and stir in. Return the pan with the
remainder of the oil to heat. Sprinkle about 2 tablespoons of corn
meal into the remaining hot oil in the pan and brown. (This
happens quickly, less than a minute, so keep an eye on it to keep it
from burning. It's just supposed to form a nice, brown, yummy
crust on the bottom) Then pour cornbread mixture into pan, put in
the oven and bake until golden brown and center springs back
when pressed, about 20 minutes.

You can do endless variations with this recipe, adding
peppers, corn kernels, bits of sausage or bacon and other stuff. My
mama always used bacon grease instead of shortening or oil and
wouldn't be caught dead putting sugar in her cornbread, though
Yankees seem to like it sweet, so be my guest if it floats your boat.

Finger Food for Strip Poker

Some of Hot Mama's poker buddies are suddenly so broke that they can't even come up with an ante for my Friday night game. Ah but in their salad days, these bankers, brokers, real estate moguls and auto execs had so much money they thought nothing of raising you $1,000 when they couldn't even beat what was showing on the table.

They lost so often and so big to me that I managed to pay off Rancho Hot Mama and equip it with advanced solar technology that allows me to generate plenty of electricity for my own needs with some left over to sell to the power company.

So I try to be generous with them in their time of need. Since they're staunch free-market fellows, I came up with a way to let them into the game that allows them to keep their ideals intact, if not their dignity. Since they have no cash, I sell them chips in exchange for their clothes. Prices range from 10 bucks for a shoe to 100 for underpants. If they win, they can buy them back. If not, well, let's just say they get a taste of their own foreclosure and repo medicine.

One thing you can say for me, though. I might send them home naked, but no one leaves Rancho Hot Mama hungry. I've had to find thriftier ways to feed people well. Pork tenderloin is inexpensive, lean and delicious. And it warms the insides of my guests, which helps, since some of the poor dears are playing sans pants.

Roast Pork Sammies

1 ½ pound pork tenderloin (not pork loin, which is a different cut entirely)
1 tablespoon olive oil
1 teaspoon fresh garlic, minced
2 teaspoons finely chopped fresh rosemary (or 1 teaspoon dry)

Marinade:
¼ cup white wine
2 tablespoons extra virgin olive oil
1 teaspoon Dijon mustard
½ teaspoon salt

Mix together marinade ingredients, pour over tenderloin and marinate 15-60 minutes

Preheat oven to 450°f. Sprinkle garlic and rosemary over tenderloin and press into the surface.

Heat olive oil over medium-high heat in a Dutch oven or large oven-proof skillet and sear meat on all sides. Roast for 15-20 minutes until internal temperature is 140°. Let stand 10 minutes and then slice thin. Serve on buns slathered with stone-ground mustard.

Tender Muffins for Tough Times
How to talk a failed investor off the ledge

When the going gets tough, the tough bake muffins. With humble ingredients, they're inexpensive to make, and baked goods are the ultimate comfort food.

That's why Hot Mama knew just what to do when the call came in that a certain real estate magnate was perched on a girder of the Skyway Bridge, contemplating an end to it all. Like everything else, the Florida real estate industry is in the toilet, and I knew it was just a matter of time before one of my poker buddies decided life was not worth living if he lost his Lexus.

I'm dreadfully afraid of heights, so there was no way I was going to climb up there to talk to him. And besides, what would I say? "Really, you'll still be virile and attractive, even if you drive a Hyundai." Who would believe that?

No, the only thing that might make a man want to live when he's lost everything is the irresistible smell of something delicious. Fortunately, I just happened to be taking peach jam muffins out of the oven when I got the call. I put them in a basket, packed a thermos of tea, and headed for the bridge.

Within minutes of my arrival, Bernie was sitting in my car, literally eating out of my hand. These muffins might not save your life, but they will make your troubles seem smaller if you share them with a friend.

Muffins to Live For

2 cups flour
1/2 teaspoon salt
2 teaspoons baking powder
1 egg, beaten
¼ cup walnut oil
1/2 cup peach jam (marmalade works great too, or any flavor of jam)
1 1/2 cups nonfat milk

Combine dry and wet ingredients separately, then mix together just until dry ingredients are moistened. Mixture will be a bit lumpy.

Spoon into greased muffin tins or tins with cupcake papers. Bake at 400°F for 20 minutes or until surface springs back under gentle pressure from a finger.

Fat Living in Lean Times

Hot Mama's birthday always calls for celebration. In fatter times, I might have flown with friends to the southern Caribbean island of Grenada for drinks on the gorgeous black sand beach and a dinner of callaloo soup and spicy sea urchin at Cleopatra's. Later, we'd stroll to a rum shack and order one of the island's aphrodisiac drinks, say mauby or *bois bandy*.

Alas, this year, celebrations of all kinds are more humble than in years past, and my birthday was no exception. But hard times are no excuse to stop all revelry. In fact, it's more important than ever to eat, drink and carouse together to keep the blues away. This dish is festive, rich and delicious. And it rivals anything that comes out of the amazing Cleopatra's kitchen in Grenada.

Cheese Grits with Shrimp

1 pound large raw shrimp, peeled and deveined (save peels for stock, see below)
3 cups hot shrimp stock (made from shells, see next page)
½ cup cream or milk
2 tablespoons butter
¾ cup sharp cheddar cheese, shredded
¾ cup Parmesan cheese, grated
Salt and black pepper to taste
1 cup quick-cooking (not instant) grits
6 bacon slices
4 tablespoons bacon grease from bacon
½ cup finely chopped onion
½ cup finely chopped green or red bell pepper
½ cup finely chopped tomato
1 clove garlic, minced
¼ cup white wine
Lemon

Put shrimp shells in a pan with 6 cups of water and simmer over medium heat until liquid is reduced by half, about 20 minutes. Strain the liquid out and set aside.

In a large saucepan over medium heat, combine cream or milk, and shrimp stock. When it starts to bubble just a little, add butter, salt and pepper.

Add grits slowly, stirring constantly. Reduce heat to low. Cook until grits are tender and liquid is absorbed, keeping a close eye on it and stirring occasionally, about 15-20 minutes.

Stir in the cheese until melted. If the grits become too thick, slowly stir in warm stock or water to thin. Remove from heat.

Fry bacon until crisp in a large frying pan over medium-high heat. Remove from heat and place on paper towels to soak up excess grease. After it cools, chop it coarsely.

Pour bacon grease into a metal pot or bowl. Clean and dry the frying pan and return 4 tablespoons of bacon grease to it.

Add onion, garlic, tomato, and bell pepper. Sauté over medium-low heat until the onion is transparent, about 10 minutes.

Toss the shrimp with salt and pepper and add to pan. Add white wine. Cook, stirring often, until shrimp are white, about 10 minutes. Spritz with lemon.

Spoon the shrimp over the grits and top with bacon.

The Big Blow

Another damned hurricane and here I sit all alone in the dark. It's bad enough the power's out, but everyone's disappeared on me, too.

My, uh, research assistant, Horst VanderVliet, is out in his King Cab truck with its oversize tires, patrolling for damsels to rescue from rising tidewaters. My sister Nicole is volunteering at a Red Cross shelter, and Great-Aunt Maria is locked in her room, praying to Santa Barbara to spare our house.

The pounding rain and screaming wind are coming in waves now. Maria's banging on pots and pans and pleading with Santa Barbara. I can tell by the edge in her voice she's about to get ugly.

We could lose it all and be swept away, and the last thing I would see is Maria fighting the current and giving Santa Barbara the finger for not saving us.

It's time to engage the vibrational part of my being. I must summon friendly spirits now, and there's only one way to do that:

Make dinner and they will come.

Easy to say but harder to do when the electricity's out. Still, I'm a Florida girl, and I know how to ride out a hurricane with a certain aplomb.

First thing to consume is whatever needs refrigeration. I start by uncorking the emergency bottle of Spanish Rioja and slicing up the Manchego cheese.

Then I take from the freezer a nice vegetarian soup I made and froze in August, when the red peppers and sweet potatoes were at their peak. It thaws fast in the dark heat of the kitchen, and will be delicious at room temperature. I always keep a French baguette in the freezer too, along with a chunk of rich Danish butter.

Sure enough, as soon as it's all ready, the doorbell rings, and refugees from the storm come piling in.

Make-Ahead Vegetarian Soup for No Electricity Days

3 cups sweet potatoes, peeled and cut up
2 red peppers, cored and cut up
½ onion, cut up
3 cloves garlic
3 cups vegetable or chicken broth
½ cup dry white wine
Salt, pepper
Hot Mama to taste

Put all ingredients into large pot and bring to a boil. Lower heat and simmer for half an hour or until all is tender.

Let cool and puree in batches in the blender or food processor. Put 1-2 servings in small Ziplock bags; store in larger bag and freeze.

To serve, remove bags from freezer and place in room temperature water until defrosted. Pour soup from bag into bowl or mug. Dollop with hot sauce to taste, and a swirl of cream or plain Greek yogurt if it's available. Serves 4-6, depending on how good it is.

A Hot Mama for All Seasons

Recipes for Holidays and Other Celebrations

Forbidden Fruit

September is my friend Patsy Rose's favorite month. That's when the kids go back to school, and she has a chance to update her MILF website. She says she just does it for Christmas-shopping money, but I think she gets a kick out of posing naked in Big Blue, her monster pickup truck.

I like September because that's when apple season starts. I love everything about this scrumptious gift of nature, including its status as the forbidden fruit that Eve employed to seduce Adam. A bum rap, by the way, if you ask me.

An apple orchard in moonlight is a magical place for lovers to cast a spell, feeding each other freshly plucked fruits and making love in the silvery mist among the craggy trees. Here's a recipe for an apple-sausage dish that tastes delicious and looks wicked.

Apples in Flagrante Delecto

3 baking apples (Granny Smith or Macintosh)
½ cup brown sugar
½ cup orange or grapefruit juice
¼ cup rum or bourbon
1 pound of ground sausage
1 tablespoon walnut oil
1 cup minced onion
1 tablespoon butter
6 link sausages (precooked)

Preheat oven to 350□.

Cut apples in half and core. Place cut side up in a buttered pie pan.

Mix together juice and liquor and pour over apples. Sprinkle with ¼ cup brown sugar.

Bake for one hour, basting at intervals.

Brown ground sausage, drain off grease, blot, and set aside.

Over low-medium heat warm walnut oil, and sauté onions till transparent. Add tablespoon butter and cook until onions are soft and translucent. Add cooked sausage to the onions.

Transfer cooked sausage mixture to a baking dish, spreading it evenly. Set the cooked apples, cut side down and not touching, on the sausage, and insert the link sausages upright into the hollow center of the apple halves.

Sprinkle with remaining ¼ cup brown sugar. Bake for half an hour or until apples are soft.

Hot Drinks for Cool Nights

October is my favorite month. The glorious cool, crisp days; the golden, glittering trees. The smell of pumpkin and cinnamon.

And best of all, costume parties where other people do what Hot Mama does pretty much all year round: dress outrageously and have anonymous sexual encounters in odd places with masked strangers.

Rum is my autumn drink of choice. It goes perfectly with the other flavors of fall, and is especially simpatico in warm, sweet drinks — the best thing on a cool autumn night.

Don't buy that awful dark spiced stuff. Get yourself some decent gold or red rum — Appleton or Mount Gay — both are readily available and not at all expensive. You can use regular sugar, but I recommend raw cane or turbinado. Both are brown and have a rich deep, rich flavor that goes especially well with rum. Probably because they both come from sugar cane.

Rum Cozy

(per serving)
1 cup milk
2-3 teaspoons sugar
1 shot of rum
Nutmeg

Heat the milk and sugar together, stirring until sugar is melted and milk is hot but not boiling. Pour into mug, add rum, stir, and grate a dusting of fresh nutmeg on top. If you want to really get fancy, top with whipped cream first and then dust with nutmeg.

Hot Buttered Rum

(per serving)
1 cup water
2-3 teaspoons of turbinado sugar
1 shot of rum
½ teaspoon of butter
Cinnamon

Put butter in bottom of mug. Heat water and sugar, stirring to dissolve. Bring to boil and pour into mug. Add rum and stir. Sprinkle with cinnamon and serve.

Hot Spiced Cider

(per serving)
1 cup fresh apple cider
1 shot of rum
Cinnamon stick
Dash of nutmeg

Heat cider, add rum, sprinkle with nutmeg and serve with cinnamon stick.

Dinner with the Big Bad Wolf

Halloween is Hot Mama's favorite holiday. Anything can happen on All Hallow's Eve, when pagan spirits dance around roaring bonfires and masked predators prowl for succulent prey.

My financial advisor, Zander, invited me to his costume dinner party last Halloween. He has unnaturally large canines and moves with a hunter's stealth, which is what inspired my costume: a crimson hooded cape over naught but a black silk chemise with matching mask and gloves. In my basket I carried a savory dish to accompany the roast venison and other game that Zander had bagged himself.

Shortly after arriving, I felt heat at my back and warm, moist breath in my ear. A deep voice growled, "Hey there, Little Red Riding Hood." The hairs on the back of my neck stood up as Zander drew back my cape and sniffed my shoulder. "You smell good enough to eat," he said and licked my neck. Oh, Grandma, what a big tongue he had!

It was probably only the mouthwatering smells emanating from my basket that kept him from ripping off my cape with his teeth then and there. We did manage to make it through dinner before my Big Bad Wolf made a dessert of me.

Red Riding Hood's Roasted Vegetables

4 medium Yukon gold potatoes
2 red bell peppers
10-15 cloves of shallots
2 sprigs fresh or 1 teaspoon dried rosemary
Kosher salt and coarse ground pepper
Extra virgin olive oil

Place potatoes in boiling water for five minutes, then remove and allow to cool. Snip rosemary sprigs into 1-inch pieces and slice peppers in 1 ½-inch-wide strips. Cut potatoes into quarters lengthwise to form long wedges and arrange in alternating rows with peppers. Peel shallots, separating into cloves and arrange over potatoes and peppers.

Tuck rosemary into layers, drizzle generously with olive oil, sprinkle with salt and pepper and roast at 400° for 30-40 minutes until shallots are golden brown and vegetables are tender.

Smashing Pumpkins

Hot Mama loves fall above all other seasons. Everything about it appeals to the senses. The brilliant colors, the rustle of fallen leaves, the bonfires on crisp cool nights, hot cider and warm kisses. And Hot Mama loves Halloween above all other holidays. Everything about it appeals to the sybaritic impulses. The magic, the pagan lust, the masks and disguises. The pumpkins.

Times are hard these days, and even with the bounty of the fall harvest, we must remember not to waste anything. That means you can have your jack-o'-lantern for Halloween, but you'd better make soup out of it November 1.

Make lots and freeze it. You'll thank me when you take it out of the freezer some cold winter eve, zap it in the microwave and heat a baguette in the toaster oven. Serve the bread with lots of butter, and the soup piping hot with a dollop of mango chutney and a swirl of plain yogurt, sour cream or crème fraisch. Cozy and delicious comfort food.

Jack-O'-Lantern Soup

1 tablespoon walnut oil
2 tablespoons butter
1 large onion, coarsely chopped
1 medium to large pumpkin, peeled and cut into 1-inch chunks
(about 6 cups)
1 large potato, chopped
2 ½ cups vegetable broth
¼ teaspoon fresh nutmeg
1 teaspoon tarragon
2 ½ cups milk (soy, oat or nut milk works fine)
2 teaspoons lemon juice

Heat oil and butter over low-medium heat in a Dutch oven.
Add onions and cook until limp and translucent.
Add pumpkin and potatoes, cover and cook for 10 minutes,
stirring occasionally.

Add broth and seasonings. Bring to a boil then reduce heat
and simmer till veggies are tender, about 15-20 minutes
.
Cool, then blend in batches until smooth. Return to pot and
add milk. Heat through gently but do not boil. Add lemon juice,
salt and fresh-ground pepper and adjust seasonings. Serve with a
dollop of plain Greek yogurt and a sprinkle of ground nutmeg.

Give Thanks for Vegetables

Hot Mama tries hard not to start getting all humbuggish in November. But it isn't easy. Of course I'm grateful for the bounty I enjoy in this country. However, in addition to rightfully pissing off Native Americans, to me, Thanksgiving signals the kick off the Family Feud and Bad Food Season.

From now through the end of the year, some family member is going to give me grief for not driving 12 hours to sit at her table and cheerfully choke down dry turkey, gummy dressing, overcooked green beans drowning in cream of mushroom soup, and all manner of super-fatted, oversweetened dishes designed to obliterate all evidence of an actual vegetable ingredient.

People, people, people: If we were kinder to our vegetables, they would taste better. And they wouldn't add yet more girth to our torsos and sludge to our arteries.

Try making these dishes for Thanksgiving instead of candied sweet potatoes with marshmallows and your grandma's green bean casserole. Both dishes have plenty of flavor, are actually nutritious and won't have you rolling on the sofa, clutching your belly in pain after dinner.

Trust me on this. Use fresh, not canned or frozen ingredients.

Baked Butternut Squash

Fresh butternut squash
Walnut oil

Cut squash into half-inch-thick slices, spray or brush with oil and roast in 450 oven for 15-20 minutes, turning once, until squash is fork tender and starting to caramelize.

Reduce temperature to 350 , remove squash from oven, cut off peel and mash. Place squash in oiled baking dish, sprinkle with cinnamon and hot red pepper flakes (optional) and bake for 25 minutes.

Green Beans with Walnut Oil

Fresh whole green beans
Walnut oil
Rice wine vinegar (or reduced balsamic)
Fresh parmesan cheese

Clean green beans and leave whole, removing only the blunt end.

Steam 7-10 minutes until tender but still bright green.

Sprinkle with walnut oil and vinegar and toss.

Grate parmesan cheese over the top.

Can be served hot or cold.

Thanksgiving Surprise
A nontraditional holiday repast

On the night before Thanksgiving last year, I was counting up all my blessing as I relaxed and sipped Champagne from a crystal goblet. I was thankful for the half-price sale where I found the cranberry silk slip I was wearing. Of course, I was also thankful for my health, my friends and family, and all the things we take for granted every day.

But most of all, I was thankful that, for the first time in more than a decade, I didn't have to cook Thanksgiving dinner. No wrestling with a clammy carcass at 6 a.m.; no peeling, boiling, mashing or baking of root vegetables. And best of all, no hysterical trips to the store 20 minutes before the people are supposed to arrive.

Tomorrow, I thought, I'll simply show up at Nicole's house with my one dish—a cranberry, walnut and arugula salad with walnut oil and reduced balsamic—in time to have a cocktail and hear all about Uncle Buck's hernia surgery.

Ha! Who was I kidding? I arrived at Nicole's a little early for our traditional pre-dinner-party nip. After knocking and getting no answer, I opened the door. Clouds of greasy, black smoke rolled out. I found Nicole in the kitchen, drunk and sobbing, a charred bird in the sink. The only consumable fowl on the premises was Wild Turkey — and she'd already gobbled most of that.

Half an hour to pull together a Thanksgiving dinner for eight. I should have known it would come to this.

In the refrigerator, I found a slightly puckered green pepper, an onion, some garlic and vinegar. The freezer held half a bottle of Stolichnaya, a lone Italian sausage and some plastic containers of unidentified sludge. I grabbed the sausage, poured myself a nice cold shot of vodka, and went to check out the pantry.

I found some cans of red beans and tomatoes, a box of rice, a vial of saffron and some cornmeal left over from our mom's visit last year. I poured myself another shot and went outside, where I spied the last fat papaya of the season clinging to a skinny tree. I whipped up some cornbread and this sweet, savory, and hearty dish.

Red Beans and Yellow Rice with Papaya Salsa

2 tablespoons olive oil
A few strands of saffron
3 15-oz. cans of dark red (or black) beans
1 14.5 oz. can of diced, peeled tomatoes (or two cups fresh)
1 green pepper diced
½ onion diced
3 cloves garlic minced*
½ teaspoon cumin*
Pinch of cinnamon*
Pinch of cayenne*
2 cups diced papaya (or mango)
1 tablespoon rice wine vinegar
1 Italian sausage (optional)

Prepare rice according to directions. (If you're using Basmati, allow 45 minutes.) Add saffron to water after it begins to boil and stir before covering.

Toss papaya with vinegar and set aside.

Slice and fry the Italian sausage and set aside.

Heat oil over medium heat and sauté onion and green pepper about three minutes, until they begin to soften. Add garlic and cook another minute until it begins to brown. Add beans, tomatoes and seasonings. Heat through, about 15 minutes.

Serve beans over rice and garnish with sausage slices, papaya and a sprig of fresh parsley or cilantro.

Serves 6 in a pinch.

The Fish That Got Away

When I want a man who's hungry for a woman, I go fishing at the Drift Inn. It's near the port, so there are always lonely sailors looking for a drink, a meal, and some female companionship.

That's where I hooked Alejandro one night, a dashing Brazilian sea captain just in from Tierra del Fuego. He'd been at sea for weeks without even seeing a woman, and it showed in the way he devoured me with his eyes.

My body hummed and throbbed in answer, and I was tempted to serve him the whole banquet then and there. But I was really looking for a date for New Year's Eve the following evening. So we drank rum and danced, until the wood in his pants resembled Pinocchio's nose. That's when I issued my invitation for the next night before making my exit.

It's New Year's Eve, and I'm wearing a dress that clings to every curve and crevice, and stilettos that could pierce a heart. The Champagne is chilling, and I've prepared a spicy shrimp dish to arouse the senses. The doorbell rings a little early. I smile at his eagerness and keep him waiting just long enough to rev his engines a bit. Then I open the door with my sexiest smile.

Damn. It's my old friend Billy Heart, in a tuxedo, looking dejected. Before I let him in, I make him promise to leave as soon as Alejandro arrives.

Billy proceeds to kill what's left of my buzz with his long, sad tale of being stood up by the malevolent harpy he's dating. When he finally finishes, I realize Alejandro is more than an hour late. I'd still let him in if he turned up now, but the sizzling opener I planned deserves better.

I slip off my stilettos and retrieve the Champagne. Billy pops the cork while I get the shrimp from the oven and two crystal flutes from the freezer. Crisp, cool Champagne washes away the bitter taste of disappointment, and the bubbles start a party in our mouths. The spicy shrimp kicks it up a notch, and has our taste buds doing a rumba. It's hard to be gloomy when your mouth is having this much fun, and soon, we're laughing and licking our fingers.

At midnight, we open another bottle of bubbly and toast the fish that got away.

Sizzling Shrimp

1 pound jumbo shrimp, raw with the shell on
Crystal hot sauce (or sriracha)
1 tbs. fresh or 2 tbs. dried chopped (leaves only) rosemary
2 tbs. butter, very cold or frozen

Put oven rack about 6 inches from broiler and preheat oven at highest setting.

Place shrimp in single layer on rimmed cookie sheet or other shallow, flat pan. Apply hot sauce liberally. Cut up butter very small and sprinkle evenly over shrimp.

Top with rosemary. Broil 3-5 minutes until shrimp turn pink.

This dish is good with beer or Champagne, depending on your budget and what kind of party you're having.

Dip Me

No Valentine's Day would be complete without the ultimate aphrodisiac, chocolate. I love it so much, I could bathe in it, but most people are content to dip bits of fruit, cake and other confections in it.

My chocolate fondue rule, whether it's a party or an intimate date for two, is that you may not feed yourself. You must feed each other instead. It's a fabulous icebreaker for a party of strangers or a shy date.

The basic recipe is simple, just chocolate, cream and, if you like, another flavoring. Usually, the additional flavoring is liquor of some sort, but you can add coffee, peanut butter, jam even hot pepper oil or flakes if you prefer.

It's also nice to have a few extra condiments to sprinkle on after you dip for a special finish.

Chocolate Fondue

The Basics
1 lb high-quality solid chocolate (or chocolate chips)
1/4 cup cream
Dash, up to ¼ cup of flavored spirits (optional)

Melt chocolate over low heat in fondue pot or just a small pot on the stove. Heat cream and spirits (or other flavoring) slowly in a pot on the stove to a low simmer (do not boil). When heated through, whisk cream mixture into melted chocolate.

Flavored spirits:
Cream sherry (my favorite)
Galliano
Rum
Frangelico (for hazelnut flavor)
Grand Marnier (orange flavor)
Fruit-flavored brandy or jam (peach, cherry, raspberry)
Coffee

Stuff to dip:
Strawberries
Bananas
Pound cake
Pineapple
Apples
Pears
Small marshmallows

Condiments:
Shredded coconut
Crumbled nuts (pecans, walnuts, peanuts, macadamia nuts)

How to Catch a Leprechaun

Last St. Patrick's Day, Hot Mama decided to get a bit of the Irish in her. And how better than luring a leprechaun?

Everyone knows if you capture a leprechaun, he'll lead you to a pot of gold he's marked with the end of a rainbow. But only certain lasses know two other excellent reasons to set a leprechaun trap. The wee fellows are much better looking than folk artists and breakfast cereal boxes would have you believe, and they're thrillingly agile, skillful lovers with surprisingly large, uh, *magic wands*. Plus, they're cobblers by trade who make shoes to turn Ferragamo green with envy.

Legend has it that you can make a leprechaun trap with a box and a few coins, but any leprechaun worth catching is too smart—and too rich—to fall for such a cheesy trick. The things a leprechaun likes almost as much as gold are strong drink and the color green, and those make much more effective bait.

To make myself more attractive to a green-loving leprechaun, I selected a snug emerald velvet dress to match my eyes and jewelry.

Then it was on to green food. I love lush fresh greens straight from my garden, but leprechauns need something more substantial. So I decided to add my favorite split pea soup to the menu.

I'm happy to report, my plan worked like a lucky charm. The smell of the soup lured a winsome leprechaun named Cormac to my door, and the hunger in his eyes grew at the sight of my green-clad curves.

After dinner, he measured my feet for emerald slippers to match my dress. Then he took me to a field of shamrocks at the end of a double rainbow and gathered a bouquet of four-leaf clovers for me. Pots of gold littered the meadow as far as the eye could see, glittering and glowing in the sun, as he explored the hills and valleys of my verdant velvet landscape.

Lucky Soup

2 ½ cups green split peas
1/4 pound chorizo or Italian sausage (optional)
2 tablespoons olive oil
1 small onion, chopped
2 carrots, sliced
1 stalk celery, sliced
2 ½ quarts water or broth (vegetable or chicken)
2 bay leaves
1 sprig fresh or 1 teaspoon dried thyme
Freshly ground black pepper

Wash split peas thoroughly, cover with cold water and let soak overnight or boil for two minutes and let stand an hour to soften.

In a large Dutch oven, cook onions, carrots and celery in olive oil over medium heat for 5-10 minutes until onions are transparent and fragrant.

Add water or broth and stir. Drain peas and add, along with thyme and bay leaves. Bring to boil, and then lower heat, cover and simmer until peas disintegrate into a thick soup — about an hour.

Brown sausage separately in a pan or oven, slice and add to soup after it has been cooking for half an hour. Stir and add water as necessary every 10-15 minutes. Serve in heated bowls with crusty bread, lots of butter and a tossed green salad.

Cook's Note: I actually like this soup better with yellow lentils; it's prettier and a bit milder tasting. But I had to make it work for St. Patrick's Day, so there's that. Also, thanks to the late and much missed Les Silva for this recipe.

April Fool for Love

My sister Nicole is afraid of clowns, but I've always had a special place in my, uh, heart for them. A kinky place for a dirty clown who looks like Billy Bob Thornton in *Bad Santa*.

Given her fear of clowns, I was especially touched when she got me one for April Fool's Day. I'd been in a bit of a sexual funk since St. Patrick's Day. Once you've had a leprechaun, everyone else seems a little tame.

Bozo turned up at my door early evening on the first, bearing a covered dish and an envelope. The note inside simply said, "Forget leprechauns and Santa Claus. Here's dinner and a show with a real live April Fool. His name is Bozo. Love, Nicole."

He had soulful eyes, a big red nose and a sensual overbite, just like you know who. And when he pulled me to him, I was thrilled to feel a firm bulge that was almost as big as his oversize shoes.

We got to the covered dish eventually. We ate it with a salad of romaine, parmesan and walnuts and a loaf of bread for sopping up the delicious sauce, but you could serve it with baked potatoes and spoon the sauce over it.

Nicole discovered the secret ingredient in this recipe—treacle, which is pretty much the same thing as blackstrap molasses — on a trip to Canada, and it makes a sweet, rich sauce that is totally divine — no fooling!

Chicken a la Bozo

4 skinless chicken thighs (bone in or out)
2 large shallots, peeled and sliced
4 medium carrots, peeled and cut into 2-inch pieces
1 tablespoon treacle or blackstrap molasses
1 cup orange juice
2 tablespoons balsamic vinegar
1 tablespoon red wine
Hot red pepper powder or flakes (1-3 teaspoons)
Salt

Preheat oven to 400°F

Mix together treacle, orange juice, vinegar and wine in a sauce pan over medium low heat until treacle is dissolved.

Arrange thighs in casserole dish or oven pan with shallots and carrots. Pour liquid over and season with salt and red pepper to taste.

Bake uncovered for two hours, basting occasionally to keep thighs moist.

Patriot Shots

Whoever said alcohol and explosives don't mix has never enjoyed a Fourth of July celebration at Rancho Hot Mama.

A good fireworks display tickles Hot Mama's patriotic heart—and her Southern states— especially after a few red, white and blue Jell-O shooters. You can make these in star molds or plastic shot glasses arranged on a tray to resemble a flag.

Red White and Blue Jell-O Shooters

Red shooter
3oz strawberry Jell-O
6oz water
4 oz tequila
2 oz triple sec

Blue shooter
3 oz regular (not sugar-free) blueberry Jell-O
6oz water
6oz vodka

White shooter
3oz regular (not sugar-free) pina colada Jell-O
6oz water
6oz rum

Bring the water to a boil and stir in Jell-O.

Remove from heat and stir two minutes, making sure Jell-O is completely dissolved.

Stir in liquor. Pour into molds or shot glasses and chill for at least three hours.

To remove from mold, set mold in warm water for 15 seconds and then turn upside down over a plate.

Hold the Mayo

We always go a little crazy on Independence Day here at Rancho Hot Mama. Something about the combination of eating good food and setting off large explosives makes my heart swell with patriotic pride and the kind of excitement only gunpowder can trigger.

For a proper Fourth of July blowout, you must have plenty of fireworks, lots of iced tea and fried chicken, some sort of fruit pie (I adore rhubarb-apple with vanilla ice cream) and a first-rate potato salad.

I love mayonnaise to death. I love it in tuna salad, on all sandwiches, even with French fries. But if you put out a party-size platter of mayo-based potato salad on a hot July day, you could end up with a lot of sick friends instead of a freedom-loving free-for-all.

But don't despair. Even the most diehard traditionalists love this potato salad, which uses a good, flavorful extra-virgin olive oil instead of mayo. Baking instead of boiling the taters gives them a flaky texture and smoky flavor.

This dish is deceptively simple and flavorful. And it won't spoil if left out all day. I serve it on a bed of romaine lettuce, and topped with a good feta cheese. It never fails to get raves. This recipe serves 10 generously and could be a main dish for a summer dinner party if served with crusty bread and butter and maybe preceded by a nice chilled soup.

Tampa Style Greek Salad

5 large Idaho baking potatoes
6 tablespoons good virgin olive oil
2 tablespoon rice wine vinegar
2 tablespoons oregano
Coarse-ground kosher salt
Fresh-ground pepper
¼ cup feta cheese, crumbled
1 head romaine lettuce, shred half and reserve half as whole leaves
¼ cup black or assorted olives
1 fresh roasted beet, sliced
½ sweet onion, sliced into matchsticks
Anchovy (optional)

Preheat oven to 450 .
Wash and pierce potatoes and place in fully heated oven.
Immediately reduce temperature to 350 . Roast for 1 hour until just
fork tender. Remove and cool for 1-2 hours. Remove peels and
slice potatoes into large mixing bowl. They will crumble into large
flakes.

Toss potatoes with 4 tablespoons of olive oil, salt, pepper, half
of oregano and arrange in mound on bed of lettuce leaves.
Surround with shredded lettuce, beet slices, onions, olives and top
with feta and rest of oregano and a nice fat anchovy if you like.
Mix remaining oil with vinegar and drizzle over greens.

Lighten Up

How to Make Those Curves a Little Less Curvy

A Tragedy Averted

When even my "big girl" jeans are too tight to tango into, I know it's time to draw the line.

With heavy heart, I bade a fond farewell to firm baguettes and creamy cheeses. Adieu to dear fettuccine with sundried tomato cream sauce—adios to sweet, sweet carrot cake. And worst of all, goodbye forever to my supreme true love: French fries.

But suddenly, amid my sorrow, a ray of hope through yonder window broke. As if she somehow sensed my suffering, my yearning for lost love, Julia Collin Davison published an exhaustive study in *Cook's Illustrated* of how to achieve the perfect oven fry. Her secret's in the soaking.

I've taken out even more of the fat for my recipe and added the perfect flavoring for a grown-up palate. It's ridiculously simple, very hard to mess up. And these taters taste as sinful as those deep-fried golden arches spuds—but these are actually good for you and have almost no fat. They're crisp and golden on the outside, soft and succulent on the inside. And the rosemary leaves (do use leaves and not powder) add a wonderful toasty crunch.

Oven Fries with Rosemary

One potato per person
Rosemary leaves, fresh or dried
Kosher salt
Coarse-ground pepper (optional)
Virgin olive oil spray

Preheat oven to 475. Cut potatoes into French-fry strips and soak in cold water for 10 minutes. Dry well, sprinkle with salt and pepper, and spray liberally with olive oil.

Add rosemary, pepper and kosher salt and toss together in a bowl.

Spray a cookie sheet with more olive oil and spread the fries out. Don't crowd them, or they won't crisp up nicely. Roast for 15-20 minutes, turning once to brown more evenly.

Sin Without Consequences

Hot Mama is proud of her curves and wouldn't dream of sharing her body with a man who doesn't appreciate a little meat on a woman's bones. But as you know by now, I do love to celebrate pretty much everything with lots of food and drink. Halloween, Christmas, Hannukah, Kwaanza, Winter Solstice, New Year's Eve and New Year's Day all present opportunities to feast.

By the time January rolls around, I can barely squeeze into my favorite little black Chanel party dress.

That's where I draw the line.

But winter is still the time for warm, savory comfort food, and I love food too much to suffer an actual diet. What I do instead is cut most of the fat out of some of my favorite recipes. If you do it right, you can actually enhance the flavor of a dish. The only difference you'll notice is that you feel pleasantly sated instead of stuffed and bloated after eating it.

The secret to the rich flavor of this dish is in the sauce, a deep and full-bodied mélange of vegetables, herbs, spices and wine, cooked down until their essences fuse and the flavors concentrate.

It is so savory, you will not miss the ass-expanding things I eliminate in this recipe, specifically the egg and flour normally used for dredging the eggplant and the vat of oil it's usually fried in.

Roasting instead of frying the eggplant enhances and deepens its flavor with a lot less oil. And you don't need the flour, which actually obscures the delicate flavor of the eggplant and sucks up even more oil.

Trust me on this. My own mama deep fried everything that wasn't green and added a big dollop of bacon fat to everything that was. I love me some fried food, and I am here to tell you this dish is honestly better than fried eggplant. I dare you to try it.

Little Black Dress Eggplant Casserole
For Coco Chanel

2 large eggplants
Virgin olive oil spray
1 large can or six large fresh Roma tomatoes diced
Dash of sugar
1 each red and green bell pepper
1 medium onion
4-6 cloves garlic
1 cup good pitted, sliced olives (black, green or mixed)
2 teaspoons capers
1/4 cup red wine
1 tablespoon Worcestershire sauce
1 teaspoon dried oregano
1 cup fat-free ricotta cheese
1 cup fat-free or low-fat mozzarella

Preheat oven to 400°F and spray 2 cookie sheets with oil.

Slice onion, peel and mash garlic cloves, and cut peppers into quarters. Spray all with oil and arrange on cookie sheet and roast until caramelized, turning as necessary, about 10-15 minutes (garlic will take less time, so watch it carefully).

Remove from oven, cool slightly, dice and put into a pot with tomatoes, olives, capers, oregano, red wine and Worcestershire sauce.

Bring to a boil, then reduce heat and simmer, reducing liquid while eggplant cooks.

Cut eggplants into ½-inch slices, sprinkle with salt, arrange on paper towels and let sit for 15 minutes. Blot moisture, then spray both sides with oil, sprinkle with salt and pepper, arrange on cookie sheet and roast until brown, about 5-10 minutes per side.

Remove and lower oven temperature to 350.

Spray large casserole dish with olive oil and arrange a layer of eggplant on bottom. Spoon tomato sauce over that and place dollops of ricotta cheese on. Smooth with a spoon. Then do another layer of eggplant, tomato sauce and cheese. Top with mozzarella and bake until cheese is browned, about 15 minutes.

Size Me Up Size Me Down

After two months of lighter eating, my big-butt jeans are downright baggy, and Sven is starting to eye my curves with renewed appreciation. I'm now squeezing into the next size down with the help of the most useful fashion invention since hair dye: stretch denim.

Sven likes a woman with ample cushioning, but I'd like to be more svelte, so I'm still eating light.

Food is one of life's greatest pleasures, and you can still enjoy it and lose weight. In fact, I find I enjoy it more when I'm losing weight because I have to take the time to think about what I'm eating and prepare fresh food. One secret is eating lots of fresh fruits and vegetables.

You don't have to be on a diet to enjoy this salsa. It's a perfect summer party dip for tortilla chips. If you are trying to slim down, this salsa makes a fabulous fat-free sauce for grilled chicken, pork, fish, or (my favorite) steamed shrimp.

You can switch out the fruit and peppers in this easily. The important thing is to use fresh ingredients. It can be served immediately but is better after a day in the refrigerator. Allow to sit out for an hour at room temperature before serving.

Pineapple Mango Salsa

1/2 pineapple, peeled and diced (about 2 cups)
1 large mango or nectarine peeled and diced
½ medium sweet onion diced
1/2 red bell pepper diced
2-3 tablespoons fresh-squeezed lime juice
1 tablespoon minced fresh ginger
2-4 tablespoons fresh minced cilantro
½ teaspoon serrano or jalapeno pepper minced (optional)
1 tablespoon canned or bottled pineapple juice, if necessary

Toss fruit, onion, ginger and peppers together with 4 tablespoons lime juice and let mixture sit for a half hour.

Add lime juice. Add pineapple juice to thin mixture if necessary.

Eating With Passion

Each meal Hot Mama cooks is like a different lover. Some are exotic and exciting, others warm and comforting.

The more meals I cook and people I love, the more I appreciate simple and pure over complicated and artificial.

That does not mean I will ever settle for blandness, in my love or culinary life. It's just that I have come to appreciate the incredible healthfulness and array of flavor, color and texture you can enjoy in fresh, quality ingredients, prepared simply.

This recipe is not only sweet, savory, smooth, crunchy and rich. It is also quite brightly colored and delicious to all the senses.

Mango Avocado Shrimp Salad

2 mangoes, diced
2 avocadoes, diced
1 cup sweet onion, coarsely chopped
1 tablespoon walnut oil
1 tablespoon rice wine vinegar
1 tablespoon lime juice
1 pound medium to large shrimp
1 stalk celery, cut in 1-inch pieces
1 carrot, cut in 1-inch pieces
1 clove garlic, mashed
½ small onion, sliced

Steam the shrimp10-15 minutes in water with celery, carrot, onion and garlic.

Cool and then peel, devein, remove tails and cut into two pieces or more if shrimp are really large.

Toss shrimp with mangoes and avocadoes. Combine oil and vinegar and pour over mixture, tossing some more until well coated. Add lime juice, salt and pepper to taste.

Variations:

If you like it spicy, add hot red pepper flakes or powder or jalapeno.

Replace shrimp with steamed crab, lobster or sautéed dry scallops.

Acknowledgments

My deepest gratitude to Tina Engler, aka Jaid Black, and Patty Marks for taking me in when I was down and giving me a magazine to play with. And for actually paying me to write this stuff! And to Syneca Featherstone for making so many of my screwball ideas over the years ideas look good with her fabulous designs.

About the Author

Susan F Edwards has been making trouble with the written word almost since she learned to read, first by starting student newspapers at her junior high and high schools and later as editor of an alternative newspaper and founding editor of a magazine about women's sexuality, which scared the beejezus out of distributors who were happily stocking convenience stores with *Playboy* and *Hustler*. She has written television documentaries, hundreds of magazine and newspaper articles, and pretty much anything anyone would pay her for.

The Co-conspirators

Noel Smith, editor and recipe tester, and the one who can actually cook. An artist and curator, Noel has been a driving force in the arts community for decades. She also collects strange cookbooks and actually follows recipes to produce food that is not only delicious but that looks pretty on the plate. She loves experimenting with new culinary techniques and throwing dinner parties at which all the dishes and cutlery match and are arranged artfully on an honest-to-God real tablecloth.

Michael English, aka Horst VanderVliet, aka Sven the Magnificent, research assistant, model, chief taste tester. An urban planner by trade and all-around bon vivant by temperament, Michael loves good food and wine and is always careful to compliment the cook, even when the pork is dry and the potatoes are burned. He is also a gracious and decorative dinner party guest — and he does the dishes. This book would probably never have seen the light of day if Michael had not repeatedly cajoled the author to git 'er done.

Printed in Great Britain
by Amazon

33797469R00050